D0553764

LINES FOR ALL OCCASIONS

Pep Talks & Picker-Uppers

KNOCK KNOCK®

VENICE, CALIFORNIA

Created and published by Knock Knock
Distributed by Who's There, Inc.
Venice, CA 90291
knockknockstuff.com

This book is a work of humor meant solely for
entertainment purposes. Actually utilizing the
lines contained herein may be illegal or lead to
bodily injury. The publisher and anyone associated
with the production of this book do not advocate
breaking the law. In no event will Knock Knock be
liable to any reader for any damages, including
direct, indirect, incidental, special, consequential,
or punitive arising out of or in connection with the
use of the lines contained in this book. So there.

Every reasonable attempt has been made to
identify owners of copyright. Errors or omissions
will be corrected in subsequent editions.

Where specific company, product, and brand
names are cited, copyright and trademarks
associated with these names are property of
their respective owners.

ISBN: 978-160106078-5
UPC: 825703-50112-4

Contents

"Don't 'should' all over yourself."

Introduction

No matter who we are, no matter
how perfect our lives, all of us
will need a pep talk at some point.
And who better to turn to than
our family and friends? As our
near and dear look to us for words
of reassurance and wisdom, we can
find ourselves at a loss for the right
thing to say. And that's where this
book comes in. *Pep Talks and Picker-
Uppers for All Occasions* provides a line
for every encounter with someone

who's down at the mouth, whether they need a rah-rah session or a dose of reality.

As a pep-talker or picker-upper, you'll want to strive to be the Franklin D. Roosevelt ("The only thing we have to fear is fear itself") or Oprah ("It doesn't mean anything if you can't fit into your clothes") of the one-on-one speech. By spreading positivity, you lift up the downtrodden. As scholar and positivity pioneer Christopher Peterson notes in *A Primer in Positive Psychology*, "Optimism has demonstrable benefits, and pessimism has drawbacks." He goes on to list a panoply of successful traits proven to be associated with the former and terrible traits with the latter.

It's a common misperception, however, that all pep talks are positive.

If a bad situation is undeniable, will you be doing your loved one any favors by sugarcoating it? One arrow in the quiver of picker-uppers is the perspective reminder, otherwise known as "It could be worse." Are your loved ones starving? Probably not. Are they completely unloved? Not likely. If you find that someone is wallowing, sometimes a swift kick in the pants is the best course of action.

One surprising effect of helping other people rally is that it actually benefits *you*. As Norman Vincent Peale, arguably one of the first self-help gurus, states, "The person who sends out positive thoughts activates the world around him positively and draws back to himself positive results." You'll gain wisdom from giving counsel and feel good about providing a helping word—or, in some cases, you'll revel in schadenfreude (pleasure in the misery of others). As you gain a reputation as a good pep-talker, your popularity will grow and you'll be privy to primo gossip. And if you really excel, you just might become a life coach and write a book.

Pep Talks and Picker-Uppers for All Occasions delves into all the important life arenas—dreams, work, money, romance, family, and self-esteem. Some lines are tried-and-true, others are off-the-wall. Some are general enough to be used numerous times, while others speak to very specific plights. The most important tool for matching line to situation is listening. Because pep-talking requires intuition and nuance, you'll want to watch carefully for cues both verbal and nonverbal. What is this person seeking from you? What might benefit this person even though he or she may not know it? Open your ears, cock your thinking hat, and let the advice flow. Whether you excuse yourself for a well-timed bathroom trip to consult this book or commit these lines to memory, your friends and family will be the better for your expert reassurance.

There can never be too much pep or pickup in the world, and soon you will be an expert on the subject, spreading your cheer and reality checks throughout the known universe. And should you yourself be the one who requires inspiration, you can either loan the book to a friend or turn it back on yourself by replacing "you" with "I" for instant affirmations.

LIFE DREAMS

When big aspirations need big cheer

EVERYONE HAS LIFE DREAMS.
With the odds stacked against
success in competitive arenas,
aspirational friends and loved ones
will inevitably need compassion,
encouragement, and wake-up calls.

Whether their ambitions are to
play for the big leagues, sing their
way off the karaoke stage, make a
splash in the New York art world,
blog their way to a bestselling

Win It for Someone

In 1928, Notre Dame coach Knute Rockne delivered the most famous pep talk in sports history. Recalling the dying words of the All-American football star George Gipp, he encouraged the team to "win one for the Gipper." Twelve years later, the speech inspired a film starring Ronald Reagan, providing the actor with a new nickname. Reagan eventually used the phrase in his 1980 presidential campaign—winning two terms for the *new* Gipper.

book, discover the cure for Lyme disease, or govern the United States and lead the free world, it's unlikely that they'll hit the marks they set.

You have two choices for supporting these dejected, often delusional loved ones: you can keep their dreams alive, perpetuating false hope and prolonging their miseries (and, occasionally, encouraging them to greatness) or you can put their dreams in check, bringing them down to earth and letting them know it's time to get a job.

To ease their disappointments, focus on their achievements, no matter how small—perhaps their Twitter audience is up or they stole the show at the local theater production. If needed, throw in some sobering facts: only one in about 70,000 will be the next American Idol; Vincent van Gogh sold just one painting in his lifetime; and in 220 years, there have been only 44 United States presidents.

Finally, if you've tried it all, tell them that failure *is* an option. Success doesn't necessarily mean happiness. And even if they're hopeless, they can always live out their failed dreams through their children.

Sports

The Olympics will come
around again in four years.

White men can *totally* jump.

You can always take a mulligan.

The fifth concussion isn't
bad—it's the sixth that does it.

It's not who wins or loses—
it's how you play the game.

But bronze oxidizes so beautifully!

It takes a long time to master croquet.

Spud Webb was only five foot seven
and he dunked like a maniac.

You're built for distance, not speed.

———•••———

Some of the best athletes in the world
have come in second—or fifth.

———•••———

That ref must be totally blind.

———•••———

Showing up is 90 percent of the
game—and boy did you ever show up!

———•••———

Every all-star needs supporting players.

———•••———

You may not get MVP, but you've
got a chance for most improved.

———•••———

They'll play you next time, for sure!

———•••———

You're not the worst one on the team.

———•••———

There's always steroids!

Performing Arts

"Don't call us, we'll call you" is an excellent sign.

You were probably too beautiful for the part.

You'll find your niche as a character actor.

So many famous singers have bad voices!

Your wig stayed on magnificently.

The acoustics were terrible!

I could tell you knew the backstory.

With audiences, it's about quality, not quantity.

If you can make it here, you
can make it anywhere.

—————•—•—————

They'll fix it in post.

—————•—•—————

No one noticed when you
said, "To pee or not to pee."

—————•—•—————

There are lots of one-armed drummers.

Keep on Truckin'

The proverbial feel-good sentiment "Keep on truckin'" dates to the 1920s. To "truck" was slang for having sex, and "truckin'" became a two-step dance move. In 1935, the term took on new meaning with blues musician Blind Boy Fuller's "Truckin' My Blues Away." It is most associated, however, with underground comic artist R. Crumb's 1968 iconic "Keep on Truckin'" poster, which has been inspiring people to keep on keeping on ever since.

That wasn't a flub—it was
inspired improvisation.

———•◦•———

Your performance was truly interesting.

———•◦•———

There's always reality TV!

Visual Arts

You are *so* avant-garde!

———•◦•———

What a palette!

———•◦•———

It'll match someone's couch beautifully.

———•◦•———

Oh, now I see it!

———•◦•———

I can tell you used a *lot* of paint.

———•◦•———

Nobody cares about what
the critics have to say.

Scrapbooking should
totally be an art form.

———•·•———

When they said a child could
have painted it, they meant a
really precocious child.

———•·•———

Realism is *so* overrated.

———•·•———

Wow, black on black!

———•·•———

Gallerists are just failed artists.

———•·•———

All the best artists have
been social rejects.

———•·•———

Your work simultaneously
references both LeRoy Neiman
and Thomas Kinkade!

———•·•———

Performance art is an act of courage.

Tip: Try, Try Again

Do you know someone who's suffering from rejection? It's not uncommon among geniuses. Editors at the publishing house Knopf noted that Jack Kerouac's "frenetic and scrambling prose perfectly expresses the feverish travels of the Beat Generation. But is that enough? I don't think so"; Sylvia Plath's writing didn't have "enough genuine talent for us to take notice"; and Jorge Luis Borges's words were "utterly untranslatable."

Literature

Spelling counts for a lot!

———•◦•———

You may be waiting tables now,
but the Great American Novel
is yours for the taking.

———•◦•———

You don't actually have to
write to be a writer.

Nobody reads the *New Yorker* anyway.

⎯⎯•⎯⎯

The first chapter really wowed me.

⎯⎯•⎯⎯

I predict that haiku is about
to make a comeback.

⎯⎯•⎯⎯

Even J. K. Rowling gets writer's block!

⎯⎯•⎯⎯

Half the battle is keeping
your butt in the chair.

⎯⎯•⎯⎯

Your iambic pentameter
is so intuitive.

⎯⎯•⎯⎯

Someday you'll be sitting in a
folding chair watching Kate
Winslet intone your words.

⎯⎯•⎯⎯

Of course there's room in the
market for more memoirs.

What the hell do agents know?

———•••———

You look amazing in your author photo.

———•••———

Nobody got Faulkner, either.

———•••———

Self-publishing is the wave of the future.

———•••———

You could always just blog.

Science

I have no doubt that the mold
will grow tomorrow.

———•••———

That white coat makes you
look incredibly sexy.

———•••———

You'll be in school for a long time, it's
true, but when you're done, you'll make
a midlevel salary toiling in a lab.

The median age of Nobel Prize winners is 53.7—you have plenty of time!

⎯⎯•◆•⎯⎯

It takes a special person to care for lab animals.

⎯⎯•◆•⎯⎯

You put the *dish* in petri dish.

⎯⎯•◆•⎯⎯

You're working for the greater good of humankind!

⎯⎯•◆•⎯⎯

All astronauts throw up during their first foray into space.

⎯⎯•◆•⎯⎯

Most hypotheses are never proven.

⎯⎯•◆•⎯⎯

The next experiment will be the one.

⎯⎯•◆•⎯⎯

Small steps lead to great breakthroughs.

⎯⎯•◆•⎯⎯

Everybody can't cure AIDS.

Politics

You're really going to make a difference!

The voters are idiots.

All publicity is good publicity.

In ten years, no one will remember
that you cheated on your wife.

You kiss babies like nobody's business.

Just think of all the citizens who put
your signs in their front yards!

Every vote counts.

They may be waging a dirty campaign,
but you're sticking to your morals.

Polls are notoriously off.

Who wants all that
responsibility anyway?

You made your point, and
that's what counts.

You could always get appointed.

Yes We Can

After losing the 2008 New Hampshire
primary, presidential candidate Barack Obama
repurposed the old union chant "Sí, se puede"
into the rallying cry of "Yes We Can." The
phrase became the ultimate picker-upper for
dejected supporters and a touchstone for the
rest of Obama's campaign. Several companies
subsequently attempted to capitalize on the
goodwill bandwagon. The most inspired?
Ben & Jerry's "Yes Pecan" ice cream.

Now you'll be able to return
to life as a private citizen.

———•·•———

You can run again in four years.

———•·•———

There's always local politics.

———•·•———

Yes, you can!

Unrealized Aspirations

At a certain point, it's appropriate
to throw in the towel.

———•·•———

It's not about getting what you want,
it's about wanting what you have.

———•·•———

We love you whether or
not you're a success.

———•·•———

"Normal" isn't a bad thing.

God has something else in store for you.

———•—•———

Self-knowledge is more
important than achievement.

———•—•———

It's the journey, not the destination.

———•—•———

Anything that teaches
humility is a good thing.

———•—•———

There's no shame in living
with your parents.

———•—•———

Why not be a big fish in a small pond?

———•—•———

It was a long shot anyway.

———•—•———

You're not dead yet.

———•—•———

I always knew you didn't have any talent.

THE DAILY GRIND

When business isn't pleasure

TRUTH BE TOLD, THEY WOULDN'T call it work if it was fun. As Drew Carey says, "Oh, you hate your job? Why didn't you say so? There's a support group for that. It's called *everybody*, and they meet at the bar." When your loved ones whine about their 9-to-5—whether they're lacking one, dealing with horror-story bosses or coworkers, contending with terrible professions, or failing

No More Gold Watch

It's official: the company man is dead. According to a recent government study, between the ages of eighteen and forty-two baby boomers have held an average of 10.8 jobs. That number is sure to be eclipsed by the younger workforce; today's typical thirty-two-year-old American has *already* been employed by nine different companies. For dejected friends, unemployment is simply a natural by-product of the fickle trajectory of the modern career path.

time and again—remind them that they're not alone.

The Conference Board, an analysis group, found that 53 percent of Americans are dissatisfied with their jobs. Since we spend 34 percent of our adult waking lives at work, griping and demoralization are inevitable, and you'll be there to pick up the pieces.

Fortunately, almost everybody toils for pay at some point, so you can respond to complainers by referring back to your own experiences. Additionally, kvetching about the workplace—and the characters in it—is tremendous fun. Why else would a recent WorkWorries.com survey find that most employees spend one or more hours per day complaining or listening to others complain about their coworkers?

When faced with a down-at-the-mouth worker, you can spin their watercooler situations in the best possible light (e.g., a laid-off friend is facing a new opportunity), compare their affairs with others (at least they *have* a job), or point to their personal lives (i.e., what really matters). *Your* job is to provide a sympathetic ear to these whiners. What better calling is that?

Termination

It's not you, it's the economy.

<hr>

You'll be rich after the lawsuit!

<hr>

Now you can devote more
time to your hobbies.

<hr>

You haven't been fired—you've
been promoted to customer!

<hr>

Paychecks are overrated.

<hr>

You've been wanting to update
your résumé, right?

<hr>

I hear baristas get great tips.

<hr>

The simplicity movement is
really hot right now.

You've been paying into
unemployment for all these
years—now it's your turn to take.

———•◦•———

It's so much less crowded at
Costco on the weekdays.

———•◦•———

Freedom's just another word
for nothing left to lose.

———•◦•———

What I wouldn't give to
sleep in every day!

———•◦•———

You'll just pull up your dress
socks and start all over again.

———•◦•———

With your qualifications,
somebody will snap you up.

———•◦•———

Don't think of it as unemployment—
think of it as vacation with a
great new job at the end of it.

If it's not the right fit, it's
better that you move on.

———•—•———

You're not unemployed,
you're a consultant!

———•—•———

You are not defined by your job.

———•—•———

I'd be happy to be a reference for you.

———•—•———

Congratulations!

Mean Boss

Don't hate the playa,
hate the game.

———•—•———

Just put your head down
and stay out of his way.

———•—•———

Ye reap what ye sow.

You'll be her boss in no time.

Everybody knows he's incompetent.

You can always sue.

It's not you, it's her.

You're the bigger person.

What Goes Around

Do you know someone with a terrible boss?
Remind him or her that even the most powerful
tyrants get their comeuppance. The deceased
"Queen of Mean," New York hotel tycoon
Leona Helmsley, treated her staff with legend-
ary cruelty, making employees crawl and beg
to keep their jobs and allowing her Maltese
dog, Trouble, to attack them at whim. Fortunately, in 1989 she was convicted of tax fraud
and spent eighteen months in prison.

You're the best ass-kisser I know.

———•·•———

Take comfort in the fact that
you're thinner than she is.

———•·•———

You catch more flies with
honey than with vinegar.

———•·•———

You can't reason with a crazy person.

———•·•———

Pride is overrated.

———•·•———

Just think of the people
skills you're learning.

———•·•———

At least *you* can sleep at night
without medication.

———•·•———

Nobody likes a whiner.

———•·•———

Your psychic shield is transcendent.

If it's so hard to work for him, think
about how hard it must be to be him.

———•—•———

There's a special place in hell
for middle managers.

———•—•———

You can always unionize.

Awful Coworker

You're getting to the top with
honor and integrity.

———•—•———

Everybody will see his true
nature eventually.

———•—•———

She feeds on your engagement—
ignore her and she'll crawl
back into her cave.

———•—•———

There's a reason why he's
still in the mailroom.

It Could Be Worse

Stifle the complaints of whiny friends with a little perspective. According to a study based on data from the United States Bureau of Labor Statistics and the Census Bureau, the workers who actually suffer the most (based on environment, income, outlook, physical demands, and stress) are lumberjacks, dairy farmers, taxi drivers, and seamen. Garbage collectors and nuclear decontamination techs are not far behind.

The boss will see right through
her behavior before long.

───◆───

You'll be the last one standing.

───◆───

At least we have stuff to talk
about at the watercooler.

───◆───

With only one idea,
he won't get very far.

You're way more popular.

———•—•———

You don't have to live with her,
you just have to work with her.

———•—•———

There are people like that
wherever you go.

———•—•———

He'll be getting
your coffee in no time.

———•—•———

Don't take it home with you.

———•—•———

Think of her as a teacher,
and the lesson is patience.

———•—•———

Karma is a bitch.

———•—•———

He's a sad, sad man.

———•—•———

Don't hate her, pity her.

Problematic Profession

Doing any job well is noble.

———•———

Everybody has to start somewhere.

———•———

Somebody's got to clean
other people's houses.

———•———

Everyone loves a man in
a chicken uniform.

———•———

You put the *service*
in customer service.

———•———

Recycling other people's cans from their
garbage is helping to save the planet!

———•———

You're keeping a dying art alive.

———•———

The city couldn't run without
revenue from parking tickets.

Spammers give people something
to complain about.

———•◦•———

You have a 93 percent chance
of *not* getting cancer from the
chemicals you work with.

———•◦•———

As long as people eat meat, animals
will have to be slaughtered.

———•◦•———

Twitter is totally journalism!

———•◦•———

White-collar workers rule the planet.

———•◦•———

You may not be using your PhD, but
you can still call yourself doctor.

———•◦•———

Door-to-door sales brings
products to the people.

———•◦•———

If only you had a nickel for each typo
you caught on a menu, you'd be rich!

Your job would make a
great reality TV show.

No one understands how you got rich
in the stock market, but it's got to be
good for the little people somehow.

You're *my* hero!

Staying home with the kids is
the most important job of all.

Nobody knows what book editors do,
but unconsciously they appreciate it.

It's the oldest profession!

Professional Failure

You need to acknowledge failure
in order to embrace success.

You make me feel so good about myself.

———•◦•———

At a certain point, it's necessary
to accept your limitations.

———•◦•———

Failure is the most important
teacher of all.

———•◦•———

'Tis better to have tried and failed
than never to have tried at all.

Post Your Pep

Gifts are one of the best ways to pick some-
one up. The company Successories is known
for its posters of idyllic nature scenes with
inspiring captions such as "Dare to Soar:
Your Attitude Almost Always Determines Your
Altitude in Life." If someone is a complete
failure, however, you'll want to go to Despair,
Inc.; its realistic messages include "Give Up:
At Some Point, Hanging in There Just Makes
You Look Like an Even Bigger Loser."

You just peaked early.

———•———

At least you burned brightly
before you burned out.

———•———

With lower standards,
you'll achieve more.

———•———

You put the *I* in failure.

———•———

You can spin the gaps in your
résumé as life experiences.

———•———

It's too bad life doesn't
have an undo button.

———•———

Thank goodness you've got
a great fashion sense.

———•———

Your kids will have the
chances that you didn't.

Literacy is so overrated.

———•·•———

Not everybody was meant to succeed.

———•·•———

The more spectacular the
failure, the more entertaining
the story at dinner parties.

———•·•———

The American dream is
actually a nightmare.

———•·•———

Addiction is a disease!

FINANCIAL
STRAITS

When it's too much or not enough

IF MONEY MAKES THE WORLD go
'round, there are bound to be issues.
As the multi-attributed saying goes,
"I've been rich and I've been poor;
believe me, rich is better." Unfortu-
nately, only 5 percent of Americans
are in the top 5 percent wealth
bracket, and even they have their
money woes.

One key argument you'll want to
make to friends struggling with

Proud Poverty

For the world's great spiritual leaders, the pursuit of wealth is the *true* poverty. Comfort those feeling the pinch with their wise words:

> "Materialism and morality have an inverse relationship." —Gandhi

> "Money breeds greed, jealousy and other social vices. It can never bring joy." —Dalai Lama

> "It is easier for a camel to go through the eye of a needle than for a rich man to enter the kingdom of God." —Jesus

their finances is that money doesn't determine happiness, an old adage that is borne out by scientific studies. There are certain situations, however, that cut into the contentment quotient, including *truly* not having enough money to live on and having one's retirement funds wiped out at an advanced age. You'll want to be the most sensitive with these sorry individuals.

Most of us, however, are just bumping along in our diminished version of the American dream, wishing we had more than we do and pledging our allegiance to revolving credit: at the end of 2008, the national debt was close to $11 trillion, while credit card debt was almost $1 trillion. Along with the government, it appears that we're doing our part—but that doesn't make it any less stressful.

We spend a lot of time comparing our financial predicaments to others', but according to a recent Pew Research Center study, Americans overestimate the number of people enjoying the lap of luxury. Tell your loved ones that they're not alone—and if that fails, remind them that as far as money goes, you can't take it with you.

Broke

With your looks, people
will buy your dinner.

———•—•———

You should rent *The Secret*.

———•—•———

Having money is a burden.

———•—•———

You just have to be creative
when you're poor.

———•—•———

Welcome to how the other
90 percent live.

———•—•———

The great artists of the
world were all broke.

———•—•———

Money is filthy lucre.

———•—•———

You know your friends love
you for who you are.

Full pockets ruin the line of clothing.

———•—•———

You're not broke—you're a bohemian!

———•—•———

Everybody's poor when they're
young, but it takes a special
person to be poor at your age.

———•—•———

Poverty is a time-proven motivator.

———•—•———

The best things in life are free.

———•—•———

Broke is a temporary condition
but poor is a state of mind.

———•—•———

I don't look down on you.

———•—•———

They're having a sale at the dollar store.

———•—•———

Your cardboard sign is the
wittiest I've ever seen.

In Debt

You'll chip away at it
slowly, like a mortgage.

———•·•———

Thank goodness debtor's prison
is a thing of the past.

———•·•———

Even the government is running a deficit.

———•·•———

A 29.99 percent APR isn't so bad.

———•·•———

The Lord's Prayer says, "And forgive us
our debts, as we forgive our debtors."

———•·•———

Spending money keeps the economy
afloat, even if you can't afford it.

———•·•———

It was fun while it lasted.

———•·•———

You've got good debt—other people
are saddled with bad debt.

Guilt is an unproductive
emotion generated by an
internalized disciplinarian.

———•••———

Look at it as an investment, not a burden.

———•••———

You're house poor but decor rich.

———•••———

How were you supposed to know
what a balloon mortgage was?

Famously Bankrupt

Many successful individuals have had their
financial ups and downs—including bankruptcy. Remind your debt-ridden friends
of the illustrious company they keep:

- P. T. Barnum
- Kim Basinger
- Walt Disney
- Ulysses S. Grant
- MC Hammer
- Larry King
- Abraham Lincoln
- Willie Nelson
- Donald Trump
- Mark Twain

Just stop answering your phone.

------•------

It was the credit card companies
that extended you the credit in
the first place. You just spent it.

------•------

Freakonomics would
exonerate you somehow.

------•------

There's always bankruptcy.

No Retirement Funds

Seventy-five is the new sixty-five.

------•------

Your investments will
rebound soon enough.

------•------

Wal-Mart hires really old
people as greeters.

------•------

At least you've got your health.

You'd be bored stiff if you
weren't working.

———•—•———

You could absolutely live on
your savings—in Uruguay.

———•—•———

Very few people invest in their
retirement until they're in their fifties.

———•—•———

Social security won't be bankrupt
for at least one more generation.

———•—•———

Your job may be outmoded, but
you're cutting edge to me.

———•—•———

You're still young enough to earn it back.

———•—•———

Meals on Wheels delivers
right to your home!

———•—•———

You'll have the opportunity to save
with all those senior discounts.

The Power of Positivity

Sometimes gifts speak louder than words. When friends are down at the mouth, buy them Rhonda Byrne's smash bestseller, *The Secret*, which asserts the ultimate positive-thinking hypothesis: if you want wealth, love, or happiness, all you have to do is imagine it and it will be yours. You might not believe in her "law of attraction," but it certainly worked for Byrne: some sources say the project has grossed over $300 million.

Working keeps you young.

———

After you're sixty-five, you can get Medicare.

———

The workforce is aging right along with you.

———

Forced retirement is an opportunity to work part-time somewhere else.

Old people who work are happier.

———•—•———

Your kids will take you in.

———•—•———

Just plan on dying young.

Can't Keep Up with the Joneses

Your net worth is not who you are.

———•—•———

Nobody can tell it's a knockoff.

———•—•———

They're probably deep in debt.

———•—•———

Their lifestyle is killing the earth.

———•—•———

Think of all the rooms they have
to pay someone to clean.

———•—•———

You can enjoy their yacht
without paying for it.

Their friendships are only
based on money.

———•———

Your Prius makes you look
better than their Escalade.

———•———

Cubic zirconia sparkles
more than diamonds.

———•———

Their kids will grow up not
knowing the value of a dollar.

———•———

You appreciate your treats
more than they do.

———•———

They shop to fill their
spiritual emptiness.

———•———

You can't eat a Fabergé egg.

———•———

She has to stay thin for her
husband to love her.

They're prisoners to their monthly nut.

———•—•———

They may have a big house, but
you have a tiny home.

———•—•———

Conspicuous consumption
is so twentieth century.

Too Rich

In fact, money *can* buy happiness.

———•—•———

I've been rich and I've been
poor, and rich is better.

———•—•———

You have so many
opportunities to give back.

———•—•———

You're learning great management
skills with all that household help.

———•—•———

You're a stimulus package in yourself.

Having a trust fund doesn't
make you a bad person.

———•———

You can always buy new friends.

———•———

They're just jealous.

———•———

Poor people have lines on their foreheads.

———•———

Museums always need a good docent.

———•———

You're an easy target.

———•———

With your tax bracket, you're keeping
a good portion of the country afloat.

———•———

People love to hate the rich, but
they just don't understand.

———•———

It must be difficult having to
refuse people all the time.

You'll get them back in your will.

———•—•———

Money is power.

———•—•———

The earth isn't going to be
destroyed in your lifetime.

———•—•———

They're all haters.

Conspicuous Austerity

Who took all the fun out of being rich? Remind
your well-to-do friends that they can have
their proletariat-chic cake and eat it too,
spending copious amounts of money on fancy
things that don't *look* expensive. Marxist
playwright Bertolt Brecht, for example, was
so self-conscious about earning money from
his 1928 hit, *The Threepenny Opera*, that he
had a brand-new, extremely expensive coat
specially tailored to look old and shabby.

ROMANTIC WOES

When love isn't in the air

LOVE HURTS, AND THEN IT HURTS some more. Whether your friends are single or coupled, active or celibate, hubba-hubbas or not-so-muches, there will be call for a pep talk or a picker-upper. If someone hasn't had their heart broken at least once, there are other, more serious things to worry about.

Painful love is such a universal experience that it's inspired a

Celebrating Singlehood

Good news for your solo friends! The stigma of singlehood is completely outdated. In the United States, singles now comprise 42 percent of adults (most children are single also) and they're the fastest-growing demographic in the country. If, however, your girlfriends are looking for love, let them know that statistically they'll fare better in Alaska (ratio: 114 single men to 100 single women) or the aptly named Paradise, Nevada (ratio: 118 to 100).

treasure trove of clichés—and they wouldn't be clichés if they weren't true. To provide the utmost in comfort, wrap your lips around "Absence makes the heart grow fonder," "It's better to have loved and lost than never to have loved at all," "The course of true love never did run smooth," or the simple but classic "It's not you, it's him [or her]."

Many single individuals idealize committed love, especially as viewed from the outside. Behind closed doors, however, the story can be very different. About 10 percent of all marriages are compromised by infidelity in any given year, while 40 percent of "'til death do us part" vows end in divorce. According to a 2008 survey by Durex, an unfortunate 44 percent of Americans are dissatisfied with their sex lives. These statistics certainly indicate that a skilled pep-talker will be in keen demand.

When love is good, however, it's so good that we're willing to risk it time and again, and when it's bad, sometimes words just aren't enough. In those cases, get out the big guns: there are few heartbreaks that a pint of ice cream or a stiff drink can't soothe, albeit temporarily.

Singlehood

You'll find it when you're not looking.

When you're ready, it will come.

There's a lid for every pot.

Being single is more fun.

You get to devote all your time to work.

If you're single, you can't get divorced.

What, your friends aren't enough?

This is your time to focus on yourself.

You have to love yourself before
someone else can love you.

Enjoy your time of freedom.

———•—•———

Love is overrated.

———•—•———

It's better to be single than to settle.

———•—•———

You won't meet someone sitting
on your couch eating ice cream.

———•—•———

You're never too old to find love.

———•—•———

Most married people are miserable.

———•—•———

You're such a catch—anybody
would be lucky to have you.

———•—•———

You cannot know what is
written in the stars.

———•—•———

You have plenty of time
to freeze your eggs.

Breakups and Rejections

There are other fish in the sea.

You have to get right back on the horse.

It's better to have loved and lost
than never to have loved at all.

Heartbreak forges character.

You were too good for her.

Your intelligence was too threatening.

He's probably out of town.

If the two of you are meant to
be, it will happen someday.

You're better off.

It's better to find out now than when
you have a mortgage and kids.

———•◦•———

I didn't want to tell you,
but I never liked her.

———•◦•———

Now you get to have breakup sex.

———•◦•———

What a great opportunity to lose weight!

Tip: Make a Mix!

There's nothing quite like a beat and lung-topping lyrics to help someone mend a broken heart. Music is guaranteed to improve one's mood (there's even an entire branch of therapy—aptly called "music therapy"—devoted to it), so make your lovelorn friends an empowering "get over it" playlist. Consider including these perhaps clichéd but time-proven hits: Gloria Gaynor's "I Will Survive" and Nancy Sinatra's "These Boots Are Made for Walkin'."

You can funnel all that energy into work.

———•———

Just because he changed his
Facebook status to single doesn't
mean he doesn't love you.

———•———

Now you can be friends!

———•———

You can't change another person,
you can only change yourself.

———•———

He's not the only person on this
planet who's going to love you.

———•———

Addicts have to hit their own bottom.

Dissatisfaction

Nobody said it would be easy.

———•———

All relationships go through
peaks and valleys.

You're just in a rut.

———•+•———

Remember—you're doing it for the kids.

———•+•———

You love each other, and
that's what counts.

———•+•———

Couples therapy works wonders.

———•+•———

It's a different kind of love.

———•+•———

You took a vow!

———•+•———

It could be worse—at least
you're not single.

———•+•———

You two just need some private time.

———•+•———

If you got divorced, you'd
have to sell the house.

Pep-Talk Professionals

When the romantic stakes are high, your encouraging words may not be enough. In these instances, recognize your limits and recommend counseling. It's a booming business—in the United States, there are more than 1.8 million people in couples therapy. Uncommitted duos are also increasingly turning to therapy *before* they tie the knot. Give your ears a break and let the professionals dish the unbiased perspective you can't provide.

Relationships take work.

Marriage is a compromise.

You've invested too much
to throw it all away.

Just be grateful
you have a partner.

You can always have an affair.

———•—•———

Dump the bastard.

———•—•———

Grow up!

Poor Sexual Performance

It happens to everyone sometimes.

———•—•———

Women are extremely hard to please.

———•—•———

It *was* good for me.

———•—•———

It gets better with practice.

———•—•———

I love your body!

———•—•———

Quality is more
important than duration.

My last relationship was
just sex—with you,
there's a deeper connection.

———•———

There's a pill for that.

———•———

It's not the size of the ship, it's
the motion in the ocean.

———•———

I would never fake it!

———•———

You just had too much to drink.

———•———

It takes time to get into
each other's rhythm.

———•———

I like it when you just lie there.

———•———

It's not you, it's me!

———•———

The first time is never good.

I'm just silent.

I love you anyway.

You're the best I've ever had!

I don't expect you to live
up to my last lover.

Sexual Drought

Celibacy is the new promiscuity.

You'll appreciate it more
when it finally happens.

It's good to take a break.

There are other ways to be close.

Everything else is so good.

You're both just tired.

———•———

Consider it revirginization.

———•———

Snuggling is very satisfying in itself.

———•———

She'll come around eventually.

———•———

All relationships go through dry spells.

———•———

It takes a while after the baby's born.

———•———

Sex is overrated.

———•———

Everybody else is having a lot
less sex than you think.

———•———

With your childhood, it's understandable.

———•———

All your best sex is ahead of you.

Your relationship is more
spiritual than carnal.

———•••———

Most couples stop after a while.

———•••———

The flames that burn the
brightest often burn out.

———•••———

Join the club!

Like Brushing Your Teeth

According to a 2008 survey by the condom
manufacturer Durex, two-thirds of Americans
believe they're not having enough sex. Encour-
age sexless friends to take a cue from the
recently published *Just Do It* and *365 Nights:
A Memoir of Intimacy*, in which the two sets of
married authors write about their commitment
to have daily sex—no matter what. These
chronicles are calls to action: just do it, a lot,
and the relationship will pick *itself* up.

FAMILY MATTERS

When nature and nurture nettle

THE GREAT ATTORNEY CLARENCE Darrow put it best: "The first half of our lives is ruined by our parents, and the second half by our children." Really, that doesn't leave time for much else. Families of origin screw us up, while the families we create bring us aggravation and heartache. One generation passes it to the next, like a grandfather clock that no longer tells time.

Dysfunctional Chic

Eschew shame and embarrassment: issues are in. The overwhelming popularity of maladjusted family memoirs, including Augusten Burroughs's *Running with Scissors*, reality TV hits such as *The Osbournes*, and daytime train wrecks like *The Jerry Springer Show* are a testament to screwed up as the new perfect—at least perfect entertainment. Help your friends capitalize on their dysfunction by encouraging them toward their fifteen minutes of fame!

Life wouldn't be interesting, however, without these dynamics. After all, it's dysfunction that forges artists and other visionaries. As Leo Tolstoy famously wrote in the opening sentence to *Anna Karenina*, "Happy families are all alike; every unhappy family is unhappy in its own way." When your loved ones complain about their relatives, remind them that very little in life bestows uniqueness like a messed-up clan. Those who actually experienced good childhoods are secretly a little jealous to be out of the loop—not to mention that they're probably suffering from unrealistic life expectations.

For those who are running the show, raising their own children, there's no winning. Kids are thankless brats constantly going through a stage or a phase, and then they move out of the house and cause empty-nest syndrome. They're most likely going to need therapy no matter their parents' intentions.

Family can love us like no one else—and they can wound us the most deeply. Whether it's following a long-distance call or a terrible-twos tantrum, pep talks and picker-uppers are in our DNA.

Disapproval

You can't live your life for somebody else.

————•—•————

They're from another generation.

————•—•————

You're making the right decisions for you.

————•—•————

They just don't understand your lifestyle.

————•—•————

You're a good person even if
you don't go to church.

————•—•————

Their judgment says more about
them than it does about you.

————•—•————

You don't need their approval—
you have to love yourself.

————•—•————

Deep down they believe you'll make
something of yourself someday.

Just because they wasted their lives
doesn't mean you need to waste yours.

———•◦•———

Look how well *their* marriage turned out.

———•◦•———

They only want the best for you.

———•◦•———

It's your choice to be fat, not theirs.

———•◦•———

They're just worried about
how you reflect on them.

———•◦•———

I think you're a really great person.

———•◦•———

You'll show them.

Lack of Support

They never learned to love.

———•◦•———

Clearly they're self-obsessed narcissists.

They may not support your
behavior, but they support you.

———•———

You're strong enough on your own.

———•———

They just don't know how to
express their love for you.

———•———

Screw them—your friends
are your support.

———•———

They just can't bear to
see you behind bars.

———•———

They never should have had children.

———•———

They cut you off for your own good.

———•———

They just aren't the touchy-feely type.

———•———

One day they'll need *you*.

You may not have their love,
but at least you'll get their money.

Try not to blame yourself.

They're WASPs—
what do you expect?

They're just not that into you.

Tip: Laugh-In

Your down-in-the-dumps relatives might
want to join a "laughing club." Started in
India by "laughter guru" Dr. Madan Kataria,
club meetings consist solely of synchronized
group laughter. It turns out laughter really *is*
contagious, and Kataria's research indicates
that giggling and guffawing—whether real
or manufactured—is good for body and soul.
When one behaves as if one were happy, the
theory goes, the mood will often follow.

Dysfunction

Congratulations on overcoming
your family of origin!

———•·•———

You'll have great material for
your multivolume memoirs.

———•·•———

It's forged your character.

———•·•———

There is no such thing as
a "normal" family.

———•·•———

At least you had something
to rebel against.

———•·•———

You wouldn't be an artist otherwise.

———•·•———

Have you thought about therapy?

———•·•———

You'll do better
with your own children.

Your empathy comes from your
experience of extreme trauma.

———

You're a superstar for breaking free.

———

You coped the best way you knew how.

———

At least the nannies loved you.

———

Thank goodness for antidepressants.

———

It's your nature to
overcome your nurture.

———

You put the *function* in dysfunctional.

Parenting Insecurities

Don't "should" all over yourself.

———

Love counts for a lot.

It's Not Their Fault

According to a 2007 UNICEF study, almost everyone in the United States has been traumatized. Topped only by England, American youths are global leaders in poor diets, low levels of physical activity, and infrequent family dinners. Americans also set the pace for exposure to violence and bullying, not to mention the number of fifteen-year-olds who smoke, drink, and have sex. Reassure struggling parents: it's not them, it's the country.

You can't compare yourself to other parents.

It's quality time, not quantity time.

You're setting a great example for your children by working at a job you love.

They won't remember the first five years anyway.

They've got a roof over their heads
and food in their bellies—
what more do they need?

———•—•———

You're a better parent than
your parents were.

———•—•———

If he didn't have a leash,
he'd run into traffic.

———•—•———

It's just as much nature as it is nurture.

———•—•———

They don't have to like you.

———•—•———

All parents worry that they're
not good enough.

———•—•———

It's more important for them to see you
happy than to have an intact family.

———•—•———

I felt the same way when
my kids were that age.

Every parent makes mistakes.

———•·•———

You hired a great nanny.

Thankless Brats

After all you've done for them, you
deserve to be taken care of.

———•·•———

Just wait until they have
their own children.

———•·•———

No good deed goes unpunished.

———•·•———

Somewhere deep down
inside, they love you.

———•·•———

They have no idea how much
horse camp costs.

———•·•———

All children take their
parents for granted.

They must be getting it
from their friends.

———•—•———

You'll be close again someday.

———•—•———

You have to be a parent, not a friend.

———•—•———

When they're on their own, they'll come
to understand the value of hard work.

———•—•———

You're not their maid!

———•—•———

You dug your own grave.

———•—•———

It's part of American culture
to disrespect one's elders.

———•—•———

If they're not mad at you, you're
not doing your job.

———•—•———

At least your marriage is still strong.

Horrible Stages and Phases

The first year is the hardest.

It's just the terrible twos.

All kids eventually get
the hang of potty-training.

It's not your fault that
your child is a biter.

Playing doctor shows a
healthy sexual curiosity.

Go easy on yourself—boys love toy
guns and girls love Cinderella.

You have to let them express themselves
through their personal appearance.

All teenagers experiment.

Peer pressure is a bitch.

If you love them, let them go.

It's hip for people in their
forties to move back in with
their parents these days.

He'll grow out of it.

Everybody Is a Winner

Millennials (AKA Generation Y), born between
1982 and 2000, are characterized by the
entitlement and confidence instilled by their
doting, reaffirming parents. With mantras
such as "You can be anything" and "You're the
best," the parental "self-esteem movement"
teaches that there's no possibility of losing or
failing. It's about time that we all jumped on the
bandwagon of assumed privilege and began to
treat *every* conversation like a pep talk.

SELF-ESTEEM

When insecurities abound

CELEBRITIES WITH TRAINERS AND waxers, retouched photographs, scripted wits on television, brainiacs using multisyllabic words— it's enough to crush one's delicate self-esteem. We live in a culture that worships greatness, especially in the arenas of attractiveness and popularity. Most of us, however, are average looking, of passable intelligence, with just enough

Hug It Out

Offering free hugs, of all things, may raise one's mood. In 2004, feeling lonely and miserable, Australian Juan Mann held up a handmade sign advertising free hugs at a local mall. A video of Mann's embrace-a-stranger act became an Internet sensation and inspired a worldwide copycat phenomenon. Mann has since appeared on *Oprah* and *Good Morning America* touting his improved self-esteem and that of millions of "Free Hugs" followers.

friends to populate a dinner party. This divide between public aspirations and private normalcy leads, naturally, to feelings of inferiority. And that's where you come in.

These days, no issue is more fraught than that of body size. Loved ones who have the misfortune to tip the scales—66 percent of American adults are overweight—will crave your encouragement as they attempt to take care of their health and fight prejudice. The list of looks insecurities is long: bald, short, big-schnozzed, acne-ridden—there are so many ways to not measure up.

Thanks to the Internet, we can now feel like outcasts in multiple venues. No longer are social groups strictly local—we see them quantified on a Facebook page. No longer are put-downs private—they're posted online. Self-esteem has a slim chance when our lives are played out in such public forums.

The total package of looks, personality, intelligence, and popularity is unachievable, and, perhaps, overrated. If happiness is the gap between expectation and reality, counsel friends to lower their standards. Good enough is good enough.

Body

Being fat doesn't mean you're not fit.

———•———

Beauty transcends size.

———•———

Your stretch marks tell the
story of your motherhood.

———•———

The more of you the merrier.

———•———

Guys with hairy backs have
the most testosterone.

———•———

Focus on what you *like* about your body.

———•———

Height doesn't matter when
you're horizontal.

———•———

Ninety-eight percent of women
worry about their bodies.

It's not weight gain, it's
postmenopausal thickening.

———•—•———

I'd give anything to have your body.

———•—•———

Even models have insecurities.

———•—•———

At a certain point in your life,
sleeveless simply isn't an option.

———•—•———

You're totally in proportion.

———•—•———

Our society is just weight obsessed.

———•—•———

It's all about carrying yourself
with confidence.

———•—•———

You're bootylicious.

———•—•———

You've got such a pretty face.

Looks

Some of the most successful people
in history have been ugly.

———•◆•———

Beauty fades; character endures.

———•◆•———

Why would you want to
look like everyone else?

———•◆•———

It's what's on the inside that counts.

———•◆•———

Your personality makes you handsome.

———•◆•———

You can always have plastic surgery.

———•◆•———

They're not wrinkles, they're laugh lines.

———•◆•———

All those celebrity photos are retouched.

———•◆•———

Women *love* bald men.

You can do so much
with makeup these days.

———◆———

You make up
for it in other ways.

———◆———

Pretty is as pretty does.

———◆———

If you were beautiful, people
would doubt your intelligence.

Don't Worry—Be Happy

When your friends are feeling blue, point them
to a new ally: positive psychology. A growing
body of research indicates that people can
boost their sense of well-being by transform-
ing their attitudes toward happiness. The
approach has rapidly gained academic and
scientific ground since its introduction in the
1990s: Positive Psychology is the most popular
course at Harvard, and similar courses are now
offered at many American colleges.

President Obama's ears stick out, too!

You look great from the back.

Picasso would have painted you.

Do you know what *jolie laide* means?

Your look will never go out of style.

I love you just the way you are.

It's the imperfections
that make you beautiful.

Your teeth are so British.

You look great for your age.

Looks don't really matter.

Personality

Your foot may always be in
your mouth, but you're hilarious.

⋅━⋅•⋅━⋅

You're not bossy, you're assertive.

⋅━⋅•⋅━⋅

Everybody loves a good pun.

⋅━⋅•⋅━⋅

You don't come across as cynical—
you project brutal realism.

⋅━⋅•⋅━⋅

Everybody else is too sensitive.

⋅━⋅•⋅━⋅

You just can't help yourself.

⋅━⋅•⋅━⋅

Self-improvement doesn't
work on everybody.

⋅━⋅•⋅━⋅

Since when is it greedy to
look out for number one?

EQ Trumps IQ

If your friend is lacking in brainpower, you won't be able to say much to convince them otherwise. Fortunately, cognitive thinking—what a typical IQ test measures—is only *one* area of intelligence. According to psychologist Daniel Goleman, IQ accounts for just 20 percent of success; emotional intelligence is where it's at. Self-awareness, self-regulation, motivation, empathy, and social skills are the sure route to leadership and respect.

You just tell it like it is.

People fall asleep when you're
talking because you make
them feel so comfortable.

You have your reasons for being a bitch.

First impressions aren't everything.

You're in therapy—that should help.

———•••———

Punch lines are overrated.

———•••———

All funny people need a straight man.

———•••———

You just need to come out of your shell.

———•••———

You're interesting when you drink.

———•••———

Your dogs love you.

Intelligence

Broad and shallow is better
than narrow and deep.

———•••———

They have calculators for that.

———•••———

You just have to try a bit
harder than others.

You're street smart!

————•————

Not everybody can be Einstein.

————•————

When you're beautiful, you
don't need to be smart.

————•————

Communication is more important
than grammar or pronunciation.

————•————

You were born in the wrong century.

————•————

People who make you feel
dumb are just insecure.

————•————

You're a really hard worker.

————•————

People who use big words are pretentious.

————•————

But you're the go-to person
for celebrity gossip!

It's your own personal style to
express opinions rather than facts.

———•◆•———

You've got a great sense of humor!

———•◆•———

With the Internet, intelligence
is less and less important.

———•◆•———

Stupid is as stupid does.

———•◆•———

You haven't let it stop you yet!

———•◆•———

Average just means you're
like most other people.

———•◆•———

That's what Wikipedia is for!

———•◆•———

A simple mind is a clear mind.

———•◆•———

They don't give Darwin
Awards to just anyone!

Ignorance is bliss.

———•◦•———

Thank goodness for the
Idiot's and *Dummies* guides!

———•◦•———

Senior moments can start
when you're quite young.

Popularity

All you need is a few good friends.

———•◦•———

Someday they'll be working
at McDonald's and you'll
be a brain surgeon.

———•◦•———

You don't get caught up
in shallow pursuits.

———•◦•———

Nobody has fun at those parties anyway.

———•◦•———

That's what your family is for.

Do you realize how much
work it is to be popular?

—————

You're above all that.

—————

When you go to the movies alone,
you can concentrate better.

—————

What, I'm not enough for you?

Tip: Talk to Yourself

It's true what they say: we can't love others
until we love ourselves. If you're the one who
needs a pep talk, use this book on yourself.
Simply replace "you" with "I": "*I* am beautiful and intelligent." "*I* am solid as a rock."
"*I* am the world's greatest pep talker." For
added effect, look in the mirror while you're
repeating the affirmations. Best of all, when
you know that *you're* special, you're better
positioned to help others!

Popular people are often the meanest.

———•———

If you get your self-esteem from
others' opinions of you, you'll
never learn to love yourself.

———•———

You're getting ahead by eating
lunch at your desk when everybody
else goes out together.

———•———

When you're true to your personality,
not everybody will like you.

———•———

You're just discriminating.

———•———

One day you'll show them.

———•———

You have so much time to read.

———•———

You'll never need to worry about
being stabbed in the back.

You just won't thank them in
your Oscar acceptance speech.

———•—•———

Dependency is a sign of weakness.

———•—•———

Your brother can always
take you to the prom.

———•—•———

They're all peaking early.

———•—•———

You've got cats.

"Freedom's just another word
for nothing left to lose."